Renal Diet Cookbook for Beginners 2020

Only Low Sodium, Low Potassium, and Low Phosphorus Healthy Recipes to Control Your Kidney Disease (CKD) and Avoid Dialysis of Kidney

Tina Cooper

ISBN: 9781709654923

Table of Contents

Introduction

If you've been diagnosed with renal disease, first, let me take a moment to share my condolences.

But after that, I would like you to know that it's not as bad as some people might make it sound like! Being diagnosed with renal disease isn't the end of the world, especially if you were diagnosed early.

Properly following a well-maintained food program, such as a Renal Diet can greatly help to decrease the progression of your disease and help you to avoid dialysis in the long run.

But always make sure to follow all the guidelines provided by your doctor before considering the Renal Diet.

What is Kidney Disease?

Before going any further, let's talk about what actually qualifies as kidney diseases. Chronic kidney diseases (known as Chronic Renal Failure/Chronic Kidney Failure) is actually a much more widespread disease than most people realize.

In fact, currently, almost 37 million American adults are living with some form of kidney disease but are completely unaware of the fact as the disease is undiagnosed.

Due to a lack of knowledge, most people fail to interpret the symptoms of renal diseases early on, and when they do, it's often too late.

Therefore, you must stay aware of the core symptoms of chronic kidney disease (CKD) as it will help you to understand if you are affected, and you can start to get proper treatment as soon as possible.

Some of the signs that you should look out for include:

- If you are having trouble concentrating or always experience fatigue, it might be because your kidneys are weak and can't filter out the impurities and toxins.

- If you are always having trouble sleeping, you might have toxins in your blood, which are causing the problem. In fact, Sleep Apnea is a very common symptom amongst individuals with chronic kidney disease.

- Healthy kidneys help to make red blood cells and remove toxins and wastes from your body while keeping your skin healthy. If you notice that you have dry and itchy skin, it might be a sign to have your kidneys checked.

- If you have the urge to urinate excessively, especially at night, your kidneys might be damaged.

- If you ever notice blood in your urine, it's an immediate sign that your kidneys are damaged. However, you should be aware that urine in the blood can also be caused by kidney stones, tumors or infections, so make sure to have your body checked as soon as possible.

- If you have difficulty urinating, it should also be considered as a sign.

- Constant lack of appetite might be a symptom of kidney disease.

- Kidney disease can lead to temperature imbalance in your body and constantly make you feel cold even in warm temperatures.

Keep in mind that these are not the only signs; there are lots of more pointers that you should keep an eye out. But regardless, if you experience any of the symptoms above for a recurring period of time, make sure to have yourself checked immediately.

What Causes Kidney Disease?

It's rather difficult to pinpoint exact actions that might cause kidney disease. Since the physiology and immunity differ from person to person, the causalities vary as well. But some of the general ones are as follows:

- People of specific ethnicity and races are more prone to have CKD, such as American Indians, Hispanics, African Americans.

- Obesity greatly increases the chance of suffering from CKD.

- Regular smoking increases the chance of CKD.

- CKD can come from natural aging.

- Having diabetes for a long time might cause CKD, as high blood sugar can damage the blood vessels in your kidneys. Almost one out of three people with diabetes are often diagnosed with CKD.

- A history of high blood pressure is one of the most common causes of kidney disease.

- If you have a history of CKD running through your family, there's a possibility that you might be affected, as well.

Understanding the Different Types of Kidney Failure

In general, there are five different kidney failures that you should know about. I will try to go through them one by one to clear things up.

The first is:

Acute Pre-Renal Kidney Failure

This is caused by insufficient blood flow to the kidney. In this scenario, the kidney fails to filter the toxins from the blood as enough blood doesn't flow through it.

It is actually possible to treat this type of failure as long your doctor is able to figure out the cause of your abnormal blood flow.

Acute Intrinsic Kidney Failure

This can happen if you experience any form of direct trauma to your kidney,s such as an accident or physical impact. This causes toxins to overload and might lead to ischemia (Oxygen fails to get enough oxygen).

Some causes include:

- Shock
- Bleeding
- Glomerulonephritis
- Renal Blood Vessel Obstruction

Chronic Pre-Renal Kidney Failure

This happens when your kidney fails to receive sufficient blood for a prolonged period of time. In this situation, the kidney tends to shrink, eventually losing its function.

Chronic Intrinsic Kidney Failure

This takes place if your kidney has experienced long-term damage due to intrinsic kidney disease.

Intrinsic diseases can come from a lack of oxygen, bleeding or trauma.

Chronic Post-Renal Kidney Failure

If you experience blockage in your urinary tract for a long time, then the pressure build-up might damage your kidney.

Understanding if Your Kidneys Have Failed

There are various ways through which you can diagnose your kidney and understand if your kidney has any problem.

Some of the common ones include:

Urinalysis

In this type of test, the doctor will take samples of your urine and check them for any abnormalities, such as sugar or abnormal protein that might have leaked into the urine.

If needed, the doctors might also perform a urinary sediment examination, which is a form of test that measures the amount of white and red cells and looks for the level of bacteria. Also, it searches for a tube-shaped particle known as cellular casts.

Urine Volume Measurements

Measuring the volume of your urine is possibly one of the simplest tests out there. If you have very low urine output, it might indicate that you have kidney disease caused by a urinary blockage.

Blood Samples

If urine isn't doing it, the doctor might ask you to take blood tests to measure out various substances that are filtered by the kidneys.

A rapid rise in levels of blood urea nitrogen or creatinine might indicate kidney failure.

Imaging

Various types of imaging tests, such as CT Scans, MRIs and Ultrasounds, tend to provide a full image of the kidney as well as the urinary tract. This allows the doctor to find blockages or abnormalities.

Kidney Tissue Samples

Tissue from your kidney can be taken and examined to look for scarring, toxin deposits or infectious organism. The physician will try to take a kidney biopsy to collect your sample.

In most cases, the doctor will take a biopsy sample while you are awake; however, the doctor will give you a local anesthetic to ensure that you don't feel any pain.

Renal Diet and its Benefits

Since the Renal Diet is generally a Low Sodium, Low Phosphorus program, there are certain health benefits that you will enjoy from this diet. (Apart from improving your kidney health). Some of the crucial ones are as follows:

- It helps to lower blood pressure
- It helps to lower your LDL cholesterol
- It helps to lower your risk of having a heart attack
- It helps to prevent heart failure
- It decreases the possibility of having a stroke
- It helps to protect your vision
- It helps to improve your memory
- It helps to lower the possibility of dementia
- It helps to build stronger bones

Among others.

What Are the Symptoms of Chronic Kidney Disease?

CKD of Chronic Kidney diseases tends to eventually get worse as time passes. The unfortunate thing, though, is that the symptoms don't really appear before the kidneys are damaged to a great extent.

During the later stages of CKD, though, as you reach almost complete kidney failure levels, you might start noticing various symptoms caused by toxin build-up in your body.

Some of the common symptoms include:

- Trouble when trying to sleep
- Breathing issues
- Abnormal urination
- Loss of appetite
- Constant feeling of nausea and vomit
- Body cramps all over
- Itching sensation all over

On the other hand, if your kidney suddenly stops working completely for some reason, you might experience more intense symptoms such as:

- Vomiting
- Rash all over
- Sudden nosebleeds
- Intense Diarrhea

- Intense Fever
- Abdominal Pain
- Back Pain

Having any one of the above-mentioned symptoms might actually be a sign that you might have a serious issue with your kidney. Instead of waiting, it's always best advised to consult with your physician as soon as possible.

Kidney Failure Treatment

If you are unfortunate enough to experience kidney failure, then you have two options.

You can look for a donor who might be able to donate one of their kidneys, or you may want to opt for dialysis.

Dialysis is an expensive and recurring process that you will need to do over and over again, depending on the condition of your kidneys.

Transplant, on the other hand, is mostly a one-time major expense, given that you are able to find a perfect match.

But regardless of the path you choose, there are thousands of people who have led a healthy and normal life, even with dialysis/kidney transplant. So, even if you are a victim, don't lose all your hopes just yet.

Let me talk a little bit about dialysis.

Dialysis is basically a process that helps to get rid of toxin and extra fluid build-up in your body through artificial means. However, an external machine won't really be able to do everything that your kidney can do, so even with dialysis; you might face some complications in the long run.

That being said, there are two types of dialysis.

Peritoneal Dialysis

This form of treatment tries to cleanse your blood by utilizing the lining of your abdominal area and cleansing solution known as "Dialysate." The best part about this dialysis is that it can easily be done at home, as long as you have a clean and private area.

Hemodialysis

This particular treatment is also known as "Hemo" and is the most common one for kidney failures. This form of dialysis utilizes a machine to filter and clean out your blood. It is recommended that you do this at a hospital; however, if you have the budget, then it is possible to do it at home, as well.

After dialysis is the kidney transplant.

Kidney Transplant

A kidney transplant, as the name implies, is essentially surgery that gives you a healthy kidney from a donor's body. It is possible to have a kidney donated from a live body or a donor who has already died but has donated their kidney for a good cause. As mentioned above, if you can get a healthy kidney, then it is possible to lead a completely normal life.

And lastly, you can try medical management.

Medical Management

If you have budget issues or j want to avoid dialysis or transplant altogether, then there are some medical solutions that you might look into to reduce the symptoms of kidney failure.

They won't completely reverse the effects, but they might let you stay healthy until your kidneys are unable to function anymore.

If you opt for medical management, then the first thing to do is consult with your physician, as they will be able to point you in the right direction.

They will create a care plan for you that will guide you on what you should do and what you should not do. Make sure to always keep a copy of the plan wherever you go and discuss the terms with your loved ones as well.

It should be noted that most individuals who tend to go for medical management opt for hospice care.

The primary aim of hospice care is to try and decrease your pain and improve the quality of your final days before you die.

In medical management, you can expect a hospice to:

- Help you by providing you with a nursing home
- Help your family and friends to support you
- Try to improve the quality of your life as much as possible
- Try to provide medications and care to help you manage your symptoms

But keep in mind that regardless of which path you take, always discuss everything with your doctor.

Learning to Deal with Kidney Failure

Learning that you are suffering from kidney failure might be a difficult thing to cope with. No matter how long you have been preparing for the inevitable, this is something that will come as a shock to you.

But, as mentioned earlier, just because you have started dialysis, doesn't mean that everything that you hold dear has to come to an end!

It might be a little bit difficult at first to get yourself oriented to a new routine, but once you get into the groove, you'll start feeling much better.

Your nurses, loved ones, doctors, and co-workers will all be there to support you.

To make things easier, though, let me break down the individual types of problems that you might face and how you can deal with them.

Stress During Kidney Failure

When you are suffering from kidney failure, it's normal to be stressed out all the time. This might lead you to skip meals or even forgetting your medication, which might affect your health even more.

But you need to understand that life is full of hurdles and setbacks, and you really can't let them hold you back.

In that light, here are six tips to help you keep your stress under control:

- Make sure to take some time to just relax and unwind. Try to practice deep breathing, visualization, meditation or even muscle relaxation. All of these will help you to stay calm and keep your body healthy.

- Make sure to involve yourself in regular exercise. Take a hike, ride a bicycle or just simply take a jog. They all help. And if those aren't your thing, then you can always go for something more soothing, like tai chi or yoga.

- When you are feeling too stressed, try to call up a friend or a beloved family member and talk to them. And if that's not helping, you can always take help from a psychiatrist/counselor.

- Try to accept the things that are not under your control, and you can't change. Trying to enforce a change on something that is not within your reach will only make things worse for you. Better advice is to look for better ways of handling the situation instead of trying to change it.

- Don't put too much pressure on yourself, try to be good to yourself and don't expect much. You are a human being, after all, right? You can make mistakes, so accept that. Just try your best.

- And lastly, always try to maintain a positive attitude. Even when things go completely wrong, try to see the good instead of the bad and focus on that. Try to find things in all phases of your life that make you happy and that you appreciate, such as your friends, work, health and family, for example. You have no idea how much help a simple change of perspective can bring.

And on the topic of working out.

Exercise

Apart from the special diet, such as the Renal Diet, physical activity is another way through which you can improve the quality of your life.

This might be a little bit tough to do if you are alone, but it is very much possible. However, you should keep in mind that working out alone won't help you; you must work out and follow a well-balanced, healthy diet.

Both of these combined will go to great lengths to help you lose weight and control your disease.

In fact, a study has shown that people who try to complete 10,1000 steps per day and work out for about 2½ hours every week, while cutting down 500-800 calories per day and following a proper diet routine, have a 50% chance of reducing blood sugar to normal levels, which will further help you to stay healthy.

Common forms of exercise include:

- Stair climbing
- Tai Chi
- Stretching
- Yoga
- Cycling
- Walking
- Swimming

And so on.

To perform these normal workouts, you don't have to join a gym or even buy any sort of expensive equipment! You can simply take a walk around your streets, do yoga at home, and so on.

Just make sure to consult with your doctor to find out which exercise is suitable for you and adjust them to your dialysis routine.

Anxiety and Depression

These two are possibly the most prominent issues that you are going to face. A feeling of depression might last for a long period of time if left unattended. Anxiety might come at the same time, but it won't last for long.

Either way, mood swings will occur that will suddenly make you sad.

However, you should know that it is completely normal to feel anxious or sad when you're going through such a huge change in life. This is even more prominent if you start taking dialysis, as it will require you to completely change your daily routine and follow a different type of diet.

During this adjusting phase, you'll feel many emotions, such as anger, fear, sadness, etc.

To summarize:

The symptoms of depression are:

- Loss of interest
- Loss of any appetite
- Sleeping problems

On the other hand, symptoms of anxiety are:

- Constant sweating
- Quick breathing
- Inconsistent heartbeat
- Constant troubling thoughts

Regardless, the main thing to know is that you are not alone in this fight. Thousands of people have and are going through the same experience. Many people often feel left alone and lose the will to fight, but it doesn't have to be the same for you.

Help is always available! Try sharing with your family members, join support groups, talk to a social worker, etc.

It doesn't matter what your situation is; if you just reach out to the right person, then you will always find the help and support that you need.

Is it Possible to Work During Dialysis?

Some people often think that you have to stop working or retire from your job the moment you start taking dialysis. But that's not necessarily true.

It is very much possible to keep working even after you start dialysis. In fact, it is recommended that you try to continue working in order to stay happier and healthier.

If your company provides health insurance, then you can even keep enjoying the benefits of insurance while you work. It will help you bear the costs of your dialysis as well.

There are some types of dialysis that provide more flexible treatment options, allowing you to have more time during the day for your job.

Nocturnal (Night-Time) dialysis, either at home or hospital, is perfect for these.

However, if you do start working during your dialysis, you should understand your limits. While you are working, it is possible that you might feel a bit weak or tired.

If you are following peritoneal dialysis, then you are going to need a clean place to do all your exchanges.

Alternatively, if you are on Hemo, then it is strictly prohibited for you to lift heavy objects or put excess pressure on your vascular access arm.

Depending on your dialysis type, you must talk to your social worker/doctor to adjust your dialysis routine and talk to your employer in order to reach an agreement.

Worst case scenario, if you are unable to work, you still have some options! Various federal and private programs will help you to have a stable income while keeping your insurance for your dialysis program.

Talk to your personal social worker in order to apply for these facilities.

What to Eat and What to Avoid in the Renal Diet

When it comes to the renal diet and keeping your kidneys healthy, the most important thing to keep in mind is to avoid foods that are high in:

- Potassium
- Phosphorus
- Sodium

That being said, the following food groups are strictly prohibited during a renal diet:

- Vitamin and mineral supplements
- Cheese
- Cream soup
- Dried beans/peas
- Ice cream
- Milk/coconut milk
- Nuts, low salt snack foods
- Peanut butter
- Nut butter
- Nutella

But don't be alarmed! There is still a bucket load of amazing ingredients that you can use to create awesome meals. These include:

Meat and Meat Substitutes

- Beef
- Chicken
- Fish
- Lamb
- Tuna
- Turkey
- Veal
- Pork Chops
- Tofu

Vegetables

- Beets
- Arugula
- Celery
- Chiles
- Carrots
- Asparagus
- Bean sprouts
- Chives
- Coleslaw
- Corn
- Cucumber
- Eggplants
- Endive
- Ginger root
- Green beans
- Lettuce
- Onions
- Parsley
- Radishes
- Spaghetti squash
- Turnips
- Vegetable, mixed
- Water chestnuts

Fruits

- Apricots
- Grapefruit
- Lime
- Pears
- Tangerines
- Apples

- Blackberries
- Peaches
- Pineapple
- Watermelon
- Cherries
- Figs
- Grapes
- Peach Nectar
- Raspberries
- Plums
- Apricot nectar
- Cranberries
- Fruit cocktail
- Lemon
- Pear nectar
- Strawberries

Bread and Cereals

- Corn Chex
- English muffins
- Melba toast
- Pretzels, unsalted
- Couscous
- Grits
- Noodles
- Rice/brown/white
- Kellogg's Cornflakes
- Crackers, unsalted
- Oyster crackers
- Spaghetti
- Cheerios
- Dinner rolls
- Pita Bread
- Tortillas

Fats

- Butter
- Canola oil
- Mayonnaise
- Cream cheese
- Margarine
- Miracle Whip

- Nondairy creamer
- Olive oil

Sweets

- Animal crackers
- Angel Food cake
- Candy corn
- Chewing um
- Cotton candy
- Crispy rice treats
- Graham crackers
- Gumdrops
- Gummy Bears
- Hard candy
- Hot tamales candy
- Jell-O
- Jellybeans
- Jolly Rancher
- Lemon cake
- Lifesavers
- Marshmallows
- Newtons
- Pie
- Poundcake
- Rice cakes
- Vanilla wafers

Dairy and Dairy Alternatives

- Almond milk
- Coffee-Mate
- Mocha mix
- Rice Dream
- Rich's Coffee Rich

Others

- Jelly
- Maple syrup
- Sugar, brown/white
- Honey
- Jam
- Sugar, powdered
- Corn syrup

List of Juice and Beverages for the Renal Diet

The list above was mostly focused on solid foods. The following list will walk you through some of the beverages and juices suitable for your diet.

Beverages and Juice

- 7 Up
- Coffee
- Cream Soda
- Fruit punch
- Ginger Ale
- Grape soda
- Lemon-Lime soda
- Lemonade
- Orange soda
- Root beer
- Tea
- Apple juice
- Apple sauce
- Cranberry juice
- Cranberry sauce
- Grapefruit juice

Answers to Frequently Asked Questions

Below are some of the most common questions about CKD.

Are Sodas Bad for a Kidney?

When considering sodas, make sure that you avoid dark sodas, such as Pepsi or Coca Cola as they include phosphorus additives that are extremely harmful to your kidneys. Replace them with Cherry 7 Up, 7 Up, cream soda, ginger ale, sprite, etc. But even so, make sure to have them in very small amounts, as little as possible.

Is Cheese Allowed or Completely Forbidden?

As a rule of thumb, cheese should be avoided as it contains large amounts of phosphorus. However, there is some cheese that is lower in phosphorus, such as cream cheese, Swiss Cheese, Natural Cheese, etc. One or two ounces of those once in a while won't hurt you.

What Are Some of the Precautions That I Can Take?

There are multiple steps that you can take to protect your kidneys. Some include:

- Follow a kidney-friendly diet, such as the renal diet
- Make sure to keep your blood pressure under control
- Stop smoking
- Keep your blood glucose level under check

Is There A Permanent Cure for CKD?

Unfortunately, no. Just like Asthma, once you get affected by CKD, you can only hope to keep it under check through proper management. There is no known permanent treatment at the moment.

What Are the Most Common Medications That I Should Avoid?

Some common medications to avoid that might lead to kidney diseases include:

- Over the counter painkillers
- Laxatives
- Enemas
- Anti-Inflammatory medicines
- Food supplements
- Vitamin and herbal medications

Always make sure to consult your Nephrologist before taking any over the counter medicine that might fall into any of the above categories.

What Are Some Common Tests to Assess Kidney Functions?

Some common tests to check the condition of your kidney include:

- Blood tests that specifically look for BUN, Electrolytes and Serum Creatinine.
- Urine tests that check for Glomerular Filtration rate and Microalbumin.
- Imaging tests such as renal ultrasound, CT Scan or MRI.
- Kidney biopsy, where a small part of your kidney is removed by a needle in order to know if it is affected.

Best Advice to Avoid Dialysis

Being diagnosed with CKD can be a very scary and terrifying experience at first; however, you should rest easy knowing that it is still possible to lead a very healthy and enjoyable life with CKD with proper care. Once you are diagnosed, you can take certain steps to prolong the functioning of your kidney and improve your quality of life while delaying the need for dialysis.

Some good health practices include:

- Make sure to exercise on a daily basis
- Try to avoid smoking altogether
- Keep your diabetes in check

- Keep your blood pressure in check
- Try to stay on a job that you love doing and keep your health insurance
- Always consult with the individuals who are taking care of your health, such as your doctor and follow their advice
- Try not to overeat and keep your weight in check
- Always try to avoid adding more salt to your diet
- Try to avoid excess sugar
- Try to be socially active as it will help to lighten your mood

And above all, do the things that you love and try to stay positive all the time.

Chapter 1: Breakfast

Blackberry Pudding

Serving: 2

Prep Time: 45 minutes

Cook Time: Nil

Ingredients:

- ¼ cup chia seeds
- ½ cup blackberries, fresh
- 1 teaspoon liquid sweetener
- 1 cup coconut milk, full fat and unsweetened
- 1 teaspoon vanilla extract

How To:

1. Take the vanilla, liquid sweetener and coconut milk and add to blender
2. Process until thick
3. Add blackberries and process until smooth
4. Divide the mixture between cups and chill for 30 minutes
5. Serve and enjoy!

Nutrition (Per Serving)

- Calories: 437
- Fat: 38g
- Carbohydrates: 8g
- Protein: 8g

Simple Green Shake

Serving: 1

Prep Time: 10 minutes

Ingredients:

- ¾ cup whole milk yogurt
- 2½ cups lettuce, mix salad greens
- 1 pack stevia
- 1 tablespoon MCT oil
- 1 tablespoon chia seeds
- 1 ½ cups of water

How To:

1. Add listed ingredients to a blender
2. Blend until you have a smooth and creamy texture
3. Serve chilled and enjoy!

Nutrition (Per Serving)

- Calories: 320
- Fat: 24g
- Carbohydrates: 17g
- Protein: 10g

Green Beans and Roasted Onion

Serving: 6

Prep Time: 10 minutes

Cook Time: 15 minutes

Ingredients:

- 1 yellow onion, sliced into rings
- ½ teaspoon onion powder
- 2 tablespoons coconut flour
- 1 1/3 pounds fresh green beans, trimmed and chopped
- ½ tablespoon salt

How To:

1. Take a large bowl and mix the salt with the onion powder and coconut flour
2. Add onion rings
3. Mix well to coat
4. Spread the rings in the baking sheet, lined with parchment paper
5. Drizzle with some oil
6. Bake for 10 minutes at 400°F
7. Parboil the green beans for 3 to 5 minutes in the boiling water
8. Drain and serve the beans with the baked onion rings
9. Serve warm and enjoy!

Nutrition (Per Serving)

- Calories: 214
- Fat: 19.4g
- Carbohydrates:3.7g
- Protein: 8.3g

Fine Morning Porridge

Serving: 2

Prep Time: 15 minutes

Cook Time: Nil

Ingredients:

- 2 tablespoons coconut flour
- 2 tablespoons vanilla protein powder
- 3 tablespoons Golden Flaxseed meal
- 1 ½ cups almond milk, unsweetened
- Powdered erythritol

How To:

1. Take a bowl and mix in flaxseed meal, protein powder, coconut flour and mix well
2. Add mix to the saucepan (placed over medium heat)
3. Add almond milk and stir, let the mixture thicken
4. Add your desired amount of sweetener and serve
5. Enjoy!

Nutrition (Per Serving)

- Calories: 259
- Fat: 13g
- Carbohydrates: 5g
- Protein: 16g

Hungarian's Porridge

Serving: 2

Prep Time: 10 minutes

Cook Time: 5-10 minutes

Ingredients:

- 1 tablespoon chia seeds
- 1 tablespoon ground flaxseed
- 1/3 cup coconut cream
- ½ cup of water
- 1 teaspoon vanilla extract
- 1 tablespoon almond butter

How To:

1. Add chia seeds, coconut cream, flaxseed, water and vanilla to a small pot
2. Stir and let it sit for 5 minutes
3. Add butter and place pot over low heat
4. Keep stirring as butter melts
5. Once the porridge is hot/not boiling, pour into a bowl
6. Enjoy!
7. Add a few berries or a dash of cream for extra flavor

Nutrition (Per Serving)

- Calories: 410
- Fat: 38g
- Carbohydrates: 10g
- Protein: 6g

Awesome Nut Porridge

Serving: 4

Prep Time: 10 minutes

Cook Time: 15 minutes

Ingredients:

- 1 cup cashew nuts, raw and unsalted
- 1 cup pecan, halved
- 2 tablespoons stevia
- 4 teaspoons coconut oil, melted
- 2 cups of water

How To:

1. Chop the nuts in a food processor and form a smooth paste
2. Add water, oil, stevia to the nut paste and transfer the mix to a saucepan
3. Stir cook for 5 minutes on high heat
4. Reduce heat to low and simmer for 10 minutes
5. Serve warm and enjoy!

Nutrition (Per Serving)

- Calories: 260
- Fat: 22g
- Carbohydrates: 12g
- Protein: 6g

Zucchini and Onion Platter

Serving: 4

Prep Time: 15 minutes

Cook Time: 45 minutes

Ingredients:

- 3 large zucchini, julienned
- ½ cup basil
- 2 red onions, thinly sliced
- ¼ teaspoon salt
- 1 teaspoon cayenne pepper
- 2 tablespoons lemon juice

How To:

1. Create zucchini Zoodles by using a vegetable peeler and shaving the zucchini with peeler lengthwise until you get to the core and seeds
2. Turn zucchini and repeat until you have long strips
3. Discard seeds
4. Lay strips on cutting board and slice lengthwise to your desired thickness
5. Mix Zoodles in a bowl alongside onion, basil, and toss
6. Sprinkle salt and cayenne pepper on top
7. Drizzle lemon juice
8. Serve and enjoy!

Nutrition (Per Serving)

- Calories: 156
- Fat: 8g
- Carbohydrates: 6g
- Protein: 7g

Collard Greens Dish

Serving: 6

Prep Time: 10 minutes

Cook Time: 60 minutes

Ingredients:

- 1 tablespoon olive oil
- 3 slices of bacon, sliced
- 1 large onion, chopped
- 2 garlic cloves, minced
- 1 teaspoon salt
- 3 cups chicken broth
- 1 red pepper flake
- 1 pound fresh collard greens, cut into 2-inch pieces

How To:

1. Take a large-sized pan and place it over medium-high heat
2. Add oil and allow the oil to heat it up
3. Add bacon and cook it until crispy and remove it, crumble the bacon and add the crumbled bacon to the pan
4. Add onion and keep cooking for 5 minutes
5. Add garlic and cook until you have a nice fragrance
6. Add collard greens and keep frying until wilted, add chicken broth and season with pepper, salt, and red pepper flakes
7. Reduce the heat and cover with a lid, simmer for 45 minutes
8. Enjoy!

Nutrition (Per Serving)

- Calories: 127
- Fat: 10g
- Carbohydrates: 8g
- Protein: 4g

Simple Zucchini BBQ

Serving: 1

Prep Time: 10 minutes

Cook Time: 1 hour

Ingredients:

- Olive oil as needed
- 3 zucchini
- ½ teaspoon black pepper
- ½ teaspoon mustard
- ½ teaspoon cumin
- 1 teaspoon paprika
- 1 teaspoon garlic powder
- 1 tablespoon of sea salt
- 1-2 stevia
- 1 tablespoon chili powder

How To:

1. Preheat your oven to 300°F

2. Take a small bowl and add cayenne, black pepper, salt, garlic, mustard, paprika, chili powder, and stevia

3. Mix well

4. Slice zucchini into 1/8 inch slices and spray them with olive oil

5. Sprinkle spice blend over zucchini and bake for 40 minutes

6. Remove and flip, spray with more olive oil and leftover spice

7. Bake for 20 minutes more

8. Serve!

Nutrition (Per Serving)

- Calories: 163
- Fat: 14g
- Carbohydrates: 3g
- Protein: 8g

Bacon and Chicken Garlic Wrap

Serving: 4

Prep Time: 15 minutes

Cook Time: 10 minutes

Ingredients:

- 1 chicken fillet, cut into small cubes
- 8-9 thin slices of bacon, cut to fit cubes
- 6 garlic cloves, minced

How To:

1. Preheat your oven to 400 °F Line a baking tray with aluminum foil
2. Add minced garlic to a bowl and rub each chicken piece with it
3. Wrap a bacon piece around each garlic chicken bite
4. Secure with a toothpick
5. Transfer bites to the baking sheet, keeping a little bit of space between them
6. Bake for about 15-20 minutes until crispy
7. Serve and enjoy!

Nutrition (Per Serving)

- Calories: 260
- Fat: 19g
- Carbohydrates: 5g
- Protein: 22g

Angel Eggs

Serving: 2

Prep Time: 30 minutes

Cook Time: Nil

Ingredients:

- 4 eggs, hardboiled and peeled
- 1 tablespoon vanilla bean sweetener, sugar-free
- 2 tablespoons Keto-Friendly mayonnaise
- 1/8 teaspoon cinnamon

How To:

1. Halve the boiled eggs and scoop out the yolk
2. Place in a bowl
3. Add egg whites on a plate
4. Add sweetener, cinnamon, mayo to the egg yolks and mash them well
5. Transfer the yolk mix to white halves
6. Serve and enjoy!

Nutrition (Per Serving)

- Calories: 184
- Fat: 15g
- Carbohydrates: 1g
- Protein: 12g

Denver Omelets

Serving: 1

Prep Time: 4 minutes

Cook Time: 1 minute

Ingredients:

- 2 tablespoons almond butter
- ¼ cup onion, chopped
- ¼ cup green bell pepper, diced
- ¼ cup grape tomatoes halved
- 2 whole eggs
- ¼ cup ham, chopped

How To:

1. Take a skillet and place it over medium heat
2. Add butter and wait until the butter melts
3. Add onion and bell pepper and sauté for a few minutes
4. Take a bowl and whip eggs
5. Add the remaining ingredients and stir
6. Add sautéed onion and pepper, stir
7. Microwave the egg mix for 1 minute
8. Serve hot!

Nutrition (Per Serving)

- Calories: 605
- Fat: 46g
- Carbohydrates: 6g
- Protein: 39g

Scrambled Eggs and Pesto

Serving: 4

Prep Time: 5 minutes

Cook Time: 5 minutes

Ingredients:

- 3 large whole eggs
- 1 tablespoon almond butter
- 1 tablespoon pesto
- 2 tablespoons creamed coconut milk
- Salt and pepper as needed

How To:

1. Take a bowl and crack open your egg
2. Season with a pinch of salt and pepper
3. Pour eggs into a pan
4. Add butter and introduce heat
5. Cook on low heat and gently add pesto
6. Once the egg is cooked and scrambled, remove from the heat
7. Spoon in coconut cream and mix well
8. Turn on the heat and cook on LOW until you have a creamy texture
9. Serve and enjoy!

Nutrition (Per Serving)

- Calories: 467
- Fat: 41g
- Carbohydrates: 3g
- Protein: 20g

Lemon Broccoli

Serving: 4

Prep Time: 10 minutes

Cook Time: 15 minutes

Ingredients:

- 2 heads broccoli, separated into florets
- 2 teaspoons extra virgin olive oil
- 1 teaspoon salt
- ½ teaspoon pepper
- 1 garlic clove, minced
- ½ teaspoon lemon juice

How To:

1. Pre-heat your oven to a temperature of 400 °F
2. Take a large-sized bowl and add broccoli florets with some extra virgin olive oil, pepper, sea salt and garlic
3. Spread the broccoli out in a single even layer on a fine baking sheet
4. Bake in your pre-heated oven for about 15-20 minutes until the florets are soft enough so that they can be pierced with a fork
5. Squeeze lemon juice over them generously before serving
6. Enjoy!

Nutrition (Per Serving)

- Calories: 49
- Fat: 2g
- Carbohydrates: 4g
- Protein: 3g

Eggplant Fries

Serving: 8

Prep Time: 10 minutes

Cook Time: 15 minutes

Ingredients:

- 2 eggs
- 2 cups almond flour
- 2 tablespoons coconut oil, spray
- 2 eggplant, peeled and cut thinly
- Salt and pepper

How To:

1. Preheat your oven to 400 °F

2. Take a bowl and mix with salt and black pepper in it

3. Take another bowl and beat eggs until frothy

4. Dip the eggplant pieces into the eggs

5. Then coat them with the flour mixture

6. Add another layer of flour and egg

7. Then, take a baking sheet and grease with coconut oil on top

8. Bake for about 15 minutes

9. Serve and enjoy!

Nutrition (Per Serving)

- Calories: 212
- Fat: 15.8g
- Carbohydrates: 12.1g
- Protein: 8.6g

Pineapple Oatmeal

Serving: 5

Prep Time: 10 minutes

Cook Time: 4-8 hours

Ingredients:

- 1 cup steel-cut oats
- 4 cups unsweetened almond milk
- 2 medium apples, slashed
- 1 teaspoon coconut oil
- 1 teaspoon cinnamon
- ¼ teaspoon nutmeg
- 2 tablespoons maple syrup, unsweetened
- A drizzle of lemon juice

Directions:

1. Add the listed ingredients to a cooking pan and mix well
2. Cook on a very low flame for 8 hours or on high flame for 4 hours
3. Gently stir
4. Add your desired toppings
5. Serve and enjoy!
6. Store in the fridge for later use, make sure to add a splash of almond milk after re-heating for added flavor

Nutrition Values (Per Serving)

- Calories: 180
- Fat: 5g
- Carbohydrates: 31g
- Protein: 5g

Simple Chia Porridge

Serving: 2

Prep Time: 10 minutes

Cook Time: 5-10 minutes

Ingredients:

- 1 tablespoon chia seeds
- 1 tablespoon ground flaxseed
- 1/3 cup coconut cream
- ½ cup of water
- 1 teaspoon vanilla extract
- 1 tablespoon almond butter

How To:

1. Add chia seeds, coconut cream, flaxseed, water and vanilla to a small pot
2. Stir and let it sit for 5 minutes
3. Add almond butter and place pot over low heat
4. Keep stirring as almond butter melts
5. Once the porridge is hot/not boiling, pour into a bowl
6. Enjoy!
7. Add a few berries or a dash of cream for extra flavor

Nutrition (Per Serving)

- Calories: 410
- Fat: 38g
- Carbohydrates: 10g
- Protein: 6g

Pepperoni Omelet

Serving: 2

Prep Time: 5 minutes

Cook Time: 20 minutes

Ingredients:

- 3 eggs
- 7 pepperoni slices
- 1 teaspoon coconut cream
- Salt and freshly ground black pepper, to taste
- 1 tablespoon almond butter

How To:

1. Take a bowl and whisk eggs with all the remaining ingredients
2. Then take a skillet and heat the butter
3. Pour one quarter of the egg mixture into your skillet
4. After that, cook for 2 minutes per side
5. Repeat to use the entire batter
6. Serve warm and enjoy!

Nutrition (Per Serving)

- Calories: 141
- Fat: 11.5g
- Carbohydrates: 0.6g
- Protein: 8.9g

Scrambled Turkey Eggs

Serving: 2

Prep Time: 15 minutes

Cook Time: 15 minutes

Ingredients:

- 1 tablespoon coconut oil
- 1 medium red bell pepper, diced
- ½ medium yellow onion, diced
- ¼ teaspoon hot pepper sauce
- 3 large free-range eggs
- ¼ teaspoon black pepper, freshly ground
- ¼ teaspoon salt

How To:

1. Set a pan to medium-high heat and add coconut oil, let it heat up

2. Add onions and Saute

3. Add turkey and red pepper

4. Cook until turkey is cooked

5. Take a bowl and beat eggs, stir in salt and pepper

6. Pour eggs in the pan with turkey and gently cook and scramble eggs

7. Top with hot sauce and enjoy!

Nutrition (Per Serving)

- Calories: 435
- Fat: 30g
- Carbohydrates: 34g
- Protein: 16g

Cinnamon Flavored Baked Apple Chips

Serving: 2

Prep Time: 5 minutes

Cook Time: 2 hours

Ingredients:

- 1 teaspoon cinnamon
- 1-2 apples

How To:

1. Preheat your oven to 200 °F
2. Take a sharp knife and slice apples into thin slices
3. Discard seeds
4. Line a baking sheet with parchment paper and arrange apples on it
5. Make sure they do not overlap
6. Once done, sprinkle cinnamon over the apples
7. Bake in the oven for 1 hour
8. Flip and bake for an hour more until no longer moist
9. Serve and enjoy!

Nutrition (Per Serving)

- Calories: 147
- Fat: 0g
- Carbohydrates: 39g
- Protein: 1g

Fine Apple Slices

Serving: 4

Prep Time: 10 minutes

Cook Time: 10 minutes

Ingredients:

- 1 cup of coconut oil
- ¼ cup date paste
- 2 tablespoons ground cinnamon
- 4 Granny Smith apples, peeled and sliced, cored

Directions:

1. Take a large-sized skillet and place it over medium heat
2. Add oil and allow the oil to heat up
3. Stir cinnamon and date paste into the oil
4. Add cut up apples and cook for 5-8 minutes until crispy
5. Serve and enjoy!

Nutrition Values (Per Serving)

- Calories: 368
- Fat: 23g
- Carbohydrates: 44g
- Protein: 1g

Chapter 2: Lunch
Cauliflower Rice and Coconut

Serving: 4

Prep Time: 20 minutes

Cook Time: 20 minutes

Ingredients:

- 3 cups cauliflower, riced
- 2/3 cups full-fat coconut milk
- 1-2 teaspoons sriracha paste
- ¼- ½ teaspoon onion powder
- Salt as needed
- Fresh basil for garnish

How To:

1. Take a pan and place it over medium-low heat
2. Add all of the ingredients and stir them until fully combined
3. Cook for about 5-10 minutes, making sure that the lid is on
4. Remove the lid and keep cooking until there's no excess liquid
5. Once the rice is soft and creamy, enjoy it!

Nutrition (Per Serving)

- Calories: 95
- Fat: 7g
- Carbohydrates: 4g
- Protein: 1g

Kale and Garlic Platter

Serving: 4

Prep Time: 5 minutes

Cook Time: 10 minutes

Ingredients:

- 1 bunch kale
- 2 tablespoons olive oil
- 4 garlic cloves, minced

How To:

1. Carefully tear the kale into bite-sized portions, making sure to remove the stem
2. Discard the stems
3. Take a large-sized pot and place it over medium heat
4. Add olive oil and let the oil heat up
5. Add garlic and stir for 2 minutes
6. Add kale and cook for 5-10 minutes
7. Serve!

Nutrition (Per Serving)

- Calories: 121
- Fat: 8g
- Carbohydrates: 5g
- Protein: 4g

Blistered Beans and Almond

Serving: 4

Prep Time: 10 minutes

Cook Time: 20 minutes

Ingredients:

- 1 pound fresh green beans, ends trimmed
- 1 ½ tablespoon olive oil
- ¼ teaspoon salt
- 1 ½ tablespoons fresh dill, minced
- Juice of 1 lemon
- ¼ cup crushed almonds
- Salt as needed

How To:

1. Preheat your oven to 400 °F
2. Add in the green beans with your olive oil and also the salt
3. Then spread them in one single layer on a large-sized sheet pan
4. Roast for 10 minutes and stir nicely, then roast for another 8-10 minutes
5. Remove it from the oven and keep stirring in the lemon juice alongside the dill
6. Top it with crushed almonds, some flaky sea salt and serve

Nutrition (Per Serving)

- Calories: 347
- Fat: 16g
- Carbohydrates: 6g
- Protein: 45g

Cucumber Soup

Serving: 4

Prep Time: 14 minutes

Cook Time: Nil

Ingredients:

- 2 tablespoons garlic, minced
- 4 cups English cucumbers, peeled and diced
- ½ cup onions, diced
- 1 tablespoon lemon juice
- 1 ½ cups vegetable broth
- ½ teaspoon salt
- ¼ teaspoon red pepper flakes
- ¼ cup parsley, diced
- ½ cup Greek yogurt, plain

How To:

1. Add the listed ingredients to a blender and emulsify by blending them (except ½ cup of chopped cucumbers)
2. Blend until smooth
3. Divide the soup amongst 4 servings and top with extra cucumbers
4. Enjoy chilled!

Nutrition (Per Serving)

- Calories: 371
- Fat: 36g
- Carbohydrates: 8g
- Protein: 4g

Eggplant Salad

Serving: 3

Prep Time: 10 minutes

Cook Time: 30 minutes

Ingredients:

- 2 eggplants, peeled and sliced
- 2 garlic cloves
- 2 green bell paper, sliced, seeds removed
- ½ cup fresh parsley
- ½ cup egg-free mayonnaise
- Salt and black pepper

How To:

1. Preheat your oven to 480 °F
2. Take a baking pan and add the eggplants and black pepper
3. Bake for about 30 minutes
4. Flip the vegetables after 20 minutes
5. Then, take a bowl and add baked vegetables and all the remaining ingredients
6. Mix well
7. Serve and enjoy!

Nutrition (Per Serving)

- Calories: 196
- Fat: 108.g
- Carbohydrates: 13.4g
- Protein: 14.6g

Cajun Crab

Serving: 2

Prep Time: 10 minutes

Cook Time: 10 minutes

Ingredients:

- 1 lemon, fresh and quartered
- 3 tablespoons Cajun seasoning
- 2 bay leaves
- 4 snow crab legs, precooked and defrosted
- Golden ghee

How To:

1. Take a large pot and fill it about halfway with salted water
2. Bring the water to a boil
3. Squeeze lemon juice into a pot and toss in remaining lemon quarters
4. Add bay leaves and Cajun seasoning
5. Then season for 1 minute
6. Add crab legs and boil for 8 minutes (make sure to keep them submerged the whole time)
7. Melt ghee in the microwave and use as a dipping sauce, enjoy!

Nutrition (Per Serving)

- Calories: 643
- Fat: 51g
- Carbohydrates: 3g
- Protein: 41g

Mushroom Pork Chops

Serving: 3

Prep Time: 10 minutes

Cook Time: 40 minutes

Ingredients:

- 8 ounces mushrooms, sliced
- 1 teaspoon garlic
- 1 onion, peeled and chopped
- 1 cup egg-free mayonnaise
- 3 pork chops, boneless
- 1 teaspoon ground nutmeg
- 1 tablespoon balsamic vinegar
- ½ cup of coconut oil

How To:

1. Take a pan and place it over medium heat
2. Add oil and let it heat up
3. Add mushrooms, onions, and stir
4. Cook for 4 minutes
5. Add pork chops, season with nutmeg, garlic powder, and brown both sides
6. Transfer the pan in the oven and bake for 30 minutes at 350 °F
7. Transfer pork chops to plates and keep it warm
8. Take a pan and place it over medium heat
9. Add vinegar, mayonnaise over mushroom mix and stir for a few minutes
10. Drizzle sauce over pork chops
11. Enjoy!

Nutrition (Per Serving)

- Calories: 600
- Fat: 10g
- Carbohydrates: 8g
- Protein: 30g

Caramelized Pork Chops

Serving: 4

Prep Time: 5 minutes

Cook Time: 30 minutes

Ingredients:

- 4 pounds chuck roast
- 4 ounces green chili, chopped
- 2 tablespoons chili powder
- ½ teaspoon dried oregano
- ½ teaspoon ground cumin
- 2 garlic cloves, minced
- Salt as needed

How To:

1. Rub your chop with 1 teaspoon of pepper and 2 teaspoons of seasoning salt

2. Take a skillet and heat some oil over medium heat

3. Brown your pork chops on each side

4. Add water and onions to the pan

5. Cover and reduce the heat, simmer it for about 20 minutes

6. Turn your chops over and add the rest of the pepper and salt

7. Cover and cook until the water evaporates and the onions turn a medium brown texture

8. Remove the chops from your pan and serve with some onions on top!

Nutrition (Per Serving)

- Calories: 271
- Fat: 19g
- Carbohydrates: 4g
- Protein: 27g

Mediterranean Pork

Serving: 4

Prep Time: 10 minutes

Cook Time: 35 minutes

Ingredients:

- 4 pork chops, bone-in
- Salt and pepper to taste
- 1 teaspoon dried rosemary
- 3 garlic cloves, peeled and minced

How To:

1. Season pork chops with salt and pepper
2. Place in roasting pan
3. Add rosemary, garlic in a pan
4. Preheat your oven to 425 ° F
5. Bake for 10 minutes
6. Lower heat to 350 ° F
7. Roast for 25 minutes more
8. Slice pork and divide on plates
9. Drizzle pan juice all over
10. Serve and enjoy!

Nutrition (Per Serving)

- Calories: 165
- Fat: 2g
- Carbohydrates: 2g
- Protein: 26g

Ground Beef and Bell Peppers

Serving: 3

Prep Time: 10 minutes

Cook Time: 10 minutes

Ingredients:

- 1 onion, chopped
- 2 tablespoons coconut oil
- 1 pound ground beef
- 1 red bell pepper, diced
- 2 cups spinach, chopped
- Salt and pepper to taste

How To:

1. Take a skillet and place it over medium heat
2. Add onion and cook until slightly browned
3. Add spinach and ground beef
4. Stir fry until done
5. Take the mixture and fill up the bell peppers
6. Serve and enjoy!

Nutrition (Per Serving)

- Calories: 350
- Fat: 23g
- Carbohydrates: 4g
- Protein: 28g

Spiced Up Pork Chops

Serving: 4

Prep Time: 4 hours 10 minutes

Cook Time: 15 minutes

Ingredients:

- ¼ cup lime juice
- 4 pork rib chops
- 1 tablespoon coconut oil, melted
- 2 garlic cloves, peeled and minced
- 1 tablespoon chili powder
- 1 teaspoon ground cinnamon
- 2 teaspoons cumin
- Salt and pepper to taste
- ½ teaspoon hot pepper sauce
- Mango, sliced

How To:

1. Take a bowl and mix in lime juice, oil, garlic, cumin, cinnamon, chili powder, salt, pepper, hot pepper sauce
2. Whisk well
3. Add pork chops and toss
4. Keep it on the side and refrigerate for 4 hours
5. Pre-heat your grill to medium and transfer pork chops to a pre-heated grill
6. Grill for 7 minutes, flip and cook for 7 minutes more
7. Divide between serving platters and serve with mango slices
8. Enjoy!

Nutrition (Per Serving)

- Calories: 200
- Fat: 8g
- Carbohydrates: 3g
- Protein: 26g

Juicy Salmon Dish

Serving: 3

Prep Time: 5 minute

Cook Time: 6 minutes

Ingredients:

- ¾ cup of water
- Few sprigs of parsley, basil, tarragon, basil
- 1 pound of salmon, skin on
- 3 teaspoon of ghee
- ¼ teaspoon of salt
- ½ teaspoon of pepper
- ½ of lemon, thinly sliced
- 1 whole carrot, julienned

How To:

1. Set your pot to Sauté mode and add water and herbs
2. Place a steamer rack inside your pot and place salmon
3. Drizzle ghee on top of the salmon and season with salt and pepper
4. Cover with lemon slices
5. Lock the lid and cook on HIGH pressure for 3 minutes
6. Release the pressure naturally over 10 minutes
7. Transfer the salmon to a serving platter
8. Set your pot to Sauté mode and add vegetables
9. Cook for 1-2 minutes
10. Serve with vegetables and salmon
11. Enjoy!

Nutrition Values (Per Serving)

- Calories: 464
- Fat: 34g
- Carbohydrates: 3g
- Protein: 34g

Platter-O-Brussels

Serving: 4

Prep Time: 10 minutes

Cook Time: 20 minutes

Ingredients:

- 2 tablespoons olive oil
- 1 yellow onion, chopped
- 2 pounds Brussels sprouts, trimmed and halved
- 4 cups chicken stock
- ¼ cup coconut cream

How To:

1. Take a pot and place over medium heat
2. Add oil and let it heat up
3. Add onion and stir cook for 3 minutes
4. Add Brussels sprouts and stir, cook for 2 minutes
5. Add stock and black pepper, stir and bring to a simmer
6. Cook for 20 minutes more
7. Use an immersion blender to make the soup creamy
8. Add coconut cream and stir well
9. Ladle into soup bowls and serve
10. Enjoy!

Nutrition (Per Serving)

- Calories: 200
- Fat: 11g
- Carbohydrates: 6g
- Protein: 11g

Almond Chicken

Serving: 3

Prep Time: 15 minutes

Cook Time: 15 minutes

Ingredients:

- 2 large chicken breasts, boneless and skinless
- 1/3 cup lemon juice
- 1 ½ cups seasoned almond meal
- 2 tablespoons coconut oil
- Lemon pepper, to taste
- Parsley for decoration

How To:

1. Slice chicken breast in half
2. Pound out each half until ¼ inch thick
3. Take a pan and place over medium heat, add oil and heat it up
4. Dip each chicken breast slice into lemon juice and let it sit for 2 minutes
5. Turnover and let the other side sit for 2 minutes as well
6. Transfer to almond meal and coat both sides
7. Add coated chicken to the oil and fry for 4 minutes per side, making sure to sprinkle lemon pepper liberally
8. Transfer to a paper-lined sheet and repeat until all chicken is fried
9. Garnish with parsley and enjoy!

Nutrition (Per Serving)

- Calories: 325
- Fat: 24g
- Carbohydrates: 3g
- Protein: 16g

BlackBerry Chicken Wings

Serving: 4

Prep Time: 35 minutes

Cook Time: 50 minutes

Ingredients:

- 3 pounds chicken wings, about 20 pieces
- ½ cup blackberry chipotle jam
- Salt and pepper to taste
- ½ cup of water

How To:

1. Add water and jam to a bowl and mix well
2. Place chicken wings in a zip bag and add two-thirds of the marinade
3. Season with salt and pepper
4. Let it marinate for 30 minutes
5. Preheat your oven to 400°F
6. Prepare a baking sheet and wire rack, place chicken wings in a wire rack and bake for 15 minutes
7. Brush remaining marinade and bake for 30 minutes more
8. Enjoy!

Nutrition (Per Serving)

- Calories: 502
- Fat: 39g
- Carbohydrates: 01.8g
- Protein: 34g

Fennel and Figs Lamb

Serving: 4

Prep Time: 10 minutes

Cook Time: 40 minutes

Ingredients:

- 12 ounces lamb racks
- 2 fennel bulbs, sliced
- Salt and pepper to taste
- 2 tablespoons olive oil
- 4 figs, cut in half
- 1/8 cup apple cider vinegar
- 1 tablespoon swerve

How To:

1. Take a bowl and add the fennel, figs, vinegar, swerve, oil and toss
2. Transfer to a baking dish
3. Season with salt and pepper
4. Bake for 15 minutes at 400 °F
5. Season lamb with salt and pepper and transfer to a heated pan over medium-high heat
6. Cook for a few minutes
7. Add lamb to the baking dish with fennel and bake for 20 minutes
8. Divide between plates and serve
9. Enjoy!

Nutrition (Per Serving)

- Calories: 230
- Fat: 3g
- Carbohydrates: 5g
- Protein: 10g

Herbed Butter Pork Chops

Serving: 3

Prep Time: 5 minutes

Cook Time: 25 minutes

Ingredients:

- 1 tablespoon almond butter, divided
- 2 boneless pork chops
- Salt and pepper to taste
- 1 tablespoon dried Italian seasoning
- 1 tablespoon olive oil

How To:

1. Preheat your oven to 350 °F
2. Pat pork chops dry with a paper towel and place them in a baking dish
3. Season with salt, pepper, and Italian seasoning
4. Drizzle olive oil over pork chops
5. Top each chop with ½ tablespoon butter
6. Bake for 25 minutes
7. Transfer pork chops onto two plates and top with butter juice
8. Serve and enjoy!

Nutrition (Per Serving)

- Calories: 333
- Fat: 23g
- Carbohydrates: 1g
- Protein: 31g

Simple Rice Mushroom Risotto

Serving: 4

Prep Time: 5 minutes

Cook Time: 15 minutes

Ingredients:

- 4 ½ cups cauliflower, riced
- 3 tablespoons coconut oil
- 1 pound Portobello mushrooms, thinly sliced
- 1 pound white mushrooms, thinly sliced
- 2 shallots, diced
- ¼ cup organic vegetable broth
- Salt and pepper to taste
- 3 tablespoons chives, chopped
- 4 tablespoons almond butter

How To:

1. Use a food processor and pulse cauliflower florets until riced

2. Take a large saucepan and heat up 2 tablespoons oil over medium-high flame

3. Add mushrooms and Sauté for 3 minutes until mushrooms are tender

4. Clear saucepan of mushrooms and liquid and keep them on the side

5. Add the rest of the 1 tablespoon oil to skillet

6. Toss shallots and cook for 60 seconds

7. Add cauliflower rice, stir for 2 minutes until coated with oil

8. Add broth to riced cauliflower and stir for 5 minutes

9. Remove pot from heat and mix in mushrooms and liquid

10. Add chives, butter

11. Season with salt and pepper

12. Serve and enjoy!

Nutrition (Per Serving)

- Calories: 438
- Fat: 17g
- Carbohydrates: 15g
- Protein: 12g

Zucchini Bowl

Serving: 4

Prep Time: 10 minutes

Cook Time: 20 minutes

Ingredients:

- 1 onion, chopped
- 3 zucchini, cut into medium chunks
- 2 tablespoons coconut milk
- 2 garlic cloves, minced
- 4 cups chicken stock
- 2 tablespoons coconut oil
- Pinch of salt
- Black pepper to taste

How To:

1. Take a pot and place it over medium heat
2. Add oil and let it heat up
3. Add zucchini, garlic, onion, and stir
4. Cook for 5 minutes
5. Add stock, salt, pepper, and stir
6. Bring to a boil and lower down the heat
7. Simmer for 20 minutes.
8. Remove heat and add coconut milk
9. Use an immersion blender until smooth
10. Ladle into soup bowls and serve
11. Enjoy!

Nutrition (Per Serving)

- Calories: 160
- Fat: 2g
- Carbohydrates: 4g
- Protein: 7g

Nice Coconut Haddock

Serving: 3

Prep Time: 10 minutes

Cook Time: 12 minutes

Ingredients:

- 4 haddock fillets, 5 ounces each, boneless
- 2 tablespoons coconut oil, melted
- 1 cup coconut, shredded and unsweetened
- ¼ cup hazelnuts, ground
- Salt to taste

How To:

1. Preheat your oven to 400 °F
2. Line a baking sheet with parchment paper
3. Keep it on the side
4. Pat fish fillets with a paper towel and season with salt
5. Take a bowl and stir in hazelnuts and shredded coconut
6. Drag fish fillets through the coconut mix until both sides are coated well
7. Transfer to a baking dish
8. Brush with coconut oil
9. Bake for about 12 minutes until flaky
10. Serve and enjoy!

Nutrition (Per Serving)

- Calories: 299
- Fat: 24g
- Carbohydrates: 1g
- Protein: 20g

Chapter 3: Dinner
Lemon Sprouts

Serving: 4

Prep Time: 10 minutes

Cook Time: Nil

Ingredients:

- 1 pound Brussels sprouts, trimmed and shredded
- 8 tablespoons olive oil
- 1 lemon, juiced and zested
- Salt and pepper to taste
- ¾ cup spicy almond and seed mix

How To:

1. Take a bowl and mix in lemon juice, salt, pepper and olive oil
2. Mix well
3. Stir in shredded Brussels sprouts and toss
4. Let it sit for 10 minutes
5. Add nuts and toss
6. Serve and enjoy!

Nutrition (Per Serving)

- Calories: 382
- Fat: 36g
- Carbohydrates: 9g
- Protein: 7g

Lemon and Broccoli Platter

Serving: 6

Prep Time: 10 minutes

Cook Time: 15 minutes

Ingredients:

- 2 heads broccoli, separated into florets
- 2 teaspoons extra virgin olive oil
- 1 teaspoon salt
- ½ teaspoon black pepper
- 1 garlic clove, minced
- ½ teaspoon lemon juice

How To:

1. Preheat your oven to 400 °F
2. Take a large-sized bowl and add broccoli florets
3. Drizzle olive oil and season with pepper, salt, and garlic
4. Spread the broccoli out in a single even layer on a baking sheet
5. Bake for 15-20 minutes until fork tender
6. Squeeze lemon juice on top
7. Serve and enjoy!

Nutrition (Per Serving)

- Calories: 49
- Fat: 1.9g
- Carbohydrates: 7g
- Protein: 3g

Chicken Liver Stew

Serving: 2

Prep Time: 10 minutes

Cook Time: Nil

Ingredients:

- 10 ounces chicken livers
- 1-ounce onion, chopped
- 2 ounces sour cream
- 1 tablespoon olive oil
- Salt to taste

How To:

1. Take a pan and place it over medium heat
2. Add oil and let it heat up
3. Add onions and fry until just browned
4. Add livers and season with salt
5. Cook until livers are half cooked
6. Transfer the mix to a stew pot
7. Add sour cream and cook for 20 minutes
8. Serve and enjoy!

Nutrition (Per Serving)

- Calories: 146
- Fat: 9g
- Carbohydrates: 2g
- Protein: 15g

Mushroom Cream Soup

Serving: 4

Prep Time: 5 minutes

Cook Time: 30 minutes

Ingredients:

- 1 tablespoon olive oil
- ½ large onion, diced
- 20 ounces mushrooms, sliced
- 6 garlic cloves, minced
- 2 cups vegetable broth
- 1 cup coconut cream
- ¾ teaspoon salt
- ¼ teaspoon black pepper

How To:

1. Take a large-sized pot and place it over medium heat
2. Add onion and mushrooms in olive oil and Sauté for 10-15 minutes
3. Make sure to keep stirring it from time to time until browned evenly
4. Add garlic and Sauté for 10 minutes more
5. Add vegetable broth, coconut cream, coconut milk, black pepper, and salt
6. Bring it to a boil and reduce the temperature to low
7. Simmer for 15 minutes
8. Use an immersion blender to puree the mixture
9. Enjoy!

Nutrition (Per Serving)

- Calories: 200
- Fat: 17g
- Carbohydrates: 5g
- Protein: 4g

Garlic Soup

Serving: 10

Prep Time: 10 minutes

Cook Time: 60 minutes

Ingredients:

- 1 *tablespoon olive oil
- 2 bulbs garlic, peeled
- 3 shallots, chopped
- 1 large head cauliflower, chopped
- 6 cups vegetable broth
- Salt and pepper to taste

How To:

1. Preheat your oven to 400 °F
2. Slice ¼ inch top off the garlic bulb and place it in aluminum foil
3. Grease with olive oil and roast in the oven for 35 minutes
4. Squeeze the flesh out of the roasted garlic
5. Heat oil in a saucepan and add shallots, Saute for 6 minutes
6. Add the garlic and remaining ingredients
7. Cover the pan and reduce the heat to low
8. Let it cook for 15-20 minutes
9. Use an immersion blender to puree the mixture
10. Season soup with salt and pepper
11. Serve and enjoy!

Nutrition (Per Serving)

- Calories: 142
- Fat: 8g
- Carbohydrates: 3.4g
- Protein: 4g

Simple Lamb Chops

Serving: 3

Prep Time: 35 minutes

Cook Time: 5 minutes

Ingredients:

- ¼ cup olive oil
- ¼ cup mint, fresh and chopped
- 8 lamb rib chops
- 1 tablespoon garlic, minced
- 1 tablespoon rosemary, fresh and chopped

How To:

1. Add rosemary, garlic, mint, olive oil into a bowl and mix well

2. Keep a tablespoon of the mixture on the side for later use

3. Toss lamb chops into the marinade, letting them marinate for 30 minutes

4. Take a cast-iron skillet and place it over medium-high heat

5. Add lamb and cook for 2 minutes per side for medium-rare

6. Let the lamb rest for a few minutes and drizzle the remaining marinade

7. Serve and enjoy!

Nutrition (Per Serving)

- Calories: 566
- Fat: 40g
- Carbohydrates: 2g
- Protein: 47g

Chicken and Mushroom Stew

Serving: 4

Prep Time: 10 minutes

Cook Time: 35 minutes

Ingredients:

- 4 chicken breast halves, cut into bite-sized pieces
- 1 pound mushrooms, sliced (5-6 cups)
- 1 bunch spring onion, chopped
- 4 tablespoons olive oil
- 1 teaspoon thyme
- Salt and pepper as needed

How To:

1. Take a large deep frying pan and place it over medium-high heat
2. Add oil and let it heat up
3. Add chicken and cook for 4-5 minutes per side until slightly browned
4. Add spring onions and mushrooms, season with salt and pepper according to your taste
5. Stir
6. Cover with lid and bring the mix to a boil
7. Lower heat and simmer for 25 minutes
8. Serve!

Nutrition (Per Serving)

- Calories: 247
- Fat: 12g
- Carbohydrates: 10g
- Protein: 23g

Roasted Carrot Soup

Serving: 4

Prep Time: 10 minutes

Cook Time: 50 minutes

Ingredients:

- 8 large carrots, washed and peeled
- 6 tablespoons olive oil
- 1-quart broth
- Cayenne pepper to taste
- Salt and pepper to taste

How To:

1. Preheat your oven to 425 °F
2. Take a baking sheet and add carrots, drizzle olive oil and roast for 30-45 minutes
3. Put roasted carrots into a blender and add the broth, puree
4. Pour into saucepan and heat soup
5. Season with salt, pepper, and cayenne
6. Drizzle olive oil
7. Serve and enjoy!

Nutrition (Per Serving)

- Calories: 222
- Fat: 18g
- Net Carbohydrates: 7g
- Protein: 5g

Garlic and Butter-Flavored Cod

Serving: 3

Prep Time: 5 minutes

Cook Time: 20 minutes

Ingredients:

- 3 Cod fillets, 8 ounces each
- ¾ pound baby bok choy halved
- 1/3 cup almond butter, thinly sliced
- 1 ½ tablespoons garlic, minced
- Salt and pepper to taste

How To:

1. Preheat your oven to 400 °F
2. Cut 3 sheets of aluminum foil (large enough to fit fillet)
3. Place cod fillet on each sheet and add butter and garlic on top
4. Add bok choy, season with pepper and salt
5. Fold packet and enclose them in pouches
6. Arrange on baking sheet
7. Bake for 20 minutes
8. Transfer to a cooling rack and let them cool
9. Enjoy!

Nutrition (Per Serving)

- Calories: 355
- Fat: 21g
- Carbohydrates: 3g
- Protein: 37g

Tilapia Broccoli Platter

Serving: 2

Prep Time: 4 minutes

Cook Time: 14 minutes

Ingredients:

- 6 ounces of tilapia, frozen
- 1 tablespoon of almond butter
- 1 tablespoon of garlic, minced
- 1 teaspoon of lemon pepper seasoning
- 1 cup of broccoli florets, fresh

How To:

1. Preheat your oven to 350 °F
2. Add fish in aluminum foil packets
3. Arrange the broccoli around fish
4. Sprinkle lemon pepper on top
5. Close the packets and seal
6. Bake for 14 minutes
7. Take a bowl and add garlic and butter, mix well and keep the mixture on the side
8. Remove the packet from the oven and transfer to a platter
9. Place butter on top of the fish and broccoli, serve and enjoy!

Nutrition (Per Serving)

- Calories: 362
- Fat: 25g
- Carbohydrates: 2g
- Protein: 29g

Parsley Scallops

Serving: 4

Prep Time: 5 minutes

Cook Time: 25 minutes

Ingredients:

- 8 tablespoons almond butter
- 2 garlic cloves, minced
- 16 large sea scallops
- Salt and pepper to taste
- 1 ½ tablespoons olive oil

How To:

1. Seasons scallops with salt and pepper
2. Take a skillet and place it over medium heat, add oil and let it heat up
3. Sauté scallops for 2 minutes per side, repeat until all scallops are cooked
4. Add butter to the skillet and let it melt
5. Stir in garlic and cook for 15 minutes
6. Return scallops to skillet and stir to coat
7. Serve and enjoy!

Nutrition (Per Serving)

- Calories: 417
- Fat: 31g
- Net Carbohydrates: 5g
- Protein: 29g

Blackened Chicken

Serving: 4

Prep Time: 10 minutes

Cook Time: 10 minutes

Ingredients:

- ½ teaspoon paprika
- 1/8 teaspoon salt
- ¼ teaspoon cayenne pepper
- ¼ teaspoon ground cumin
- ¼ teaspoon dried thyme
- 1/8 teaspoon ground white pepper
- 1/8 teaspoon onion powder
- 2 chicken breasts, boneless and skinless

How To:

1. Preheat your oven to 350 °F
2. Grease baking sheet
3. Take a cast-iron skillet and place it over high heat
4. Add oil and heat it up for 5 minutes until smoking hot
5. Take a small bowl and mix salt, paprika, cumin, white pepper, cayenne, thyme, onion powder
6. Oil the chicken breast on both sides and coat the breast with the spice mix
7. Transfer to your hot pan and cook for 1 minute per side
8. Transfer to your prepared baking sheet and bake for 5 minutes
9. Serve and enjoy!

Nutrition (Per Serving)

- Calories: 136
- Fat: 3g
- Carbohydrates: 1g
- Protein: 24g

Spicy Paprika Lamb Chops

Serving: 4

Prep Time: 10 minutes

Cook Time: 15 minutes

Ingredients:

- 2 lamb racks, cut into chops
- Salt and pepper to taste
- 3 tablespoons paprika
- ¾ cup cumin powder
- 1 teaspoon chili powder

How To:

1. Take a bowl and add the paprika, cumin, chili, salt, pepper, and stir
2. Add lamb chops and rub the mixture
3. Heat grill over medium-temperature and add lamb chops, cook for 5 minutes
4. Flip and cook for 5 minutes more, flip again
5. Cook for 2 minutes, flip and cook for 2 minutes more
6. Serve and enjoy!

Nutrition (Per Serving)

- Calories: 200
- Fat: 5g
- Carbohydrates: 4g
- Protein: 8g

One-Pot Beef Roast

Serving: 4

Prep Time: 10 minutes

Cook Time: 75 minutes

Ingredients:

- 3 ½ pounds beef roast
- 4 ounces mushrooms, sliced
- 12 ounces beef stock
- 1-ounce onion soup mix
- ½ cup Italian dressing

How To:

1. Take a bowl and add the stock, onion soup mix, and Italian dressing
2. Stir
3. Put beef roast in pan
4. Add the mushrooms and stock mix to the pan and cover with foil
5. Preheat your oven to 300 °F
6. Bake for 1 hour and 15 minutes
7. Let the roast cool
8. Slice and serve
9. Enjoy the gravy on top!

Nutrition (Per Serving)

- Calories: 700
- Fat: 56g
- Carbohydrates: 10g
- Protein: 70g

Cabbage and Beef Fry

Serving: 4

Prep Time: 5 minutes

Cook Time: 15 minutes

Ingredients:

- 1 pound beef, ground
- ½ pound bacon
- 1 onion
- 1 garlic cloves, minced
- ½ head cabbage
- Salt and pepper to taste

How To:

1. Take a skillet and place it over medium heat
2. Add chopped bacon, beef and onion until slightly browned
3. Transfer to a bowl and keep it covered
4. Add minced garlic and cabbage to the skillet and cook until slightly browned
5. Return the ground beef mixture to the skillet and simmer for 3-5 minutes over low heat
6. Serve and enjoy!

Nutrition (Per Serving)

- Calories: 360
- Fat: 22g
- Net Carbohydrates: 5g
- Protein: 34g

Mushroom and Olive Sirloin Steak

Serving: 4

Prep Time: 10 minutes

Cook Time: 14 minutes

Ingredients:

- 1 pound boneless beef sirloin steak, ¾ inch thick, cut into 4 pieces
- 1 large red onion, chopped
- 1 cup mushrooms
- 4 garlic cloves, thinly sliced
- 4 tablespoons olive oil
- ½ cup green olives, coarsely chopped
- 1 cup parsley leaves, finely cut

How To:

1. Take a large-sized skillet and place it over medium-high heat
2. Add oil and let it heat p
3. Add beef and cook until both sides are browned, remove beef and drain fat
4. Add the rest of the oil to skillet and heat it up
5. Add onions, garlic and cook for 2-3 minutes
6. Stir well
7. Add mushrooms olives and cook until mushrooms are thoroughly done
8. Return beef to skillet and lower heat to medium
9. Cook for 3-4 minutes (covered)
10. Stir in parsley
11. Serve and enjoy!

Nutrition (Per Serving)

- Calories: 386
- Fat: 30g
- Carbohydrates: 11g
- Protein: 21g

Parsley and Chicken Breast

Serving: 4

Prep Time: 10 minutes

Cook Time: 40 minutes

Ingredients:

- 1 tablespoon dry parsley
- 1 tablespoon dry basil
- 4 chicken breast halves, boneless and skinless
- ½ teaspoon salt
- ½ teaspoon red pepper flakes, crushed

How To:

1. Preheat your oven to 350 °F
2. Take a 9x13 inch baking dish and grease it with cooking spray
3. Sprinkle 1 tablespoon of parsley, 1 teaspoon of basil and spread the mixture over your baking dish
4. Arrange the chicken breast halves over the dish and sprinkle garlic slices on top
5. Take a small bowl and add 1 teaspoon parsley, 1 teaspoon of basil, salt, basil, red pepper and mix well. Pour the mixture over the chicken breast
6. Bake for 25 minutes
7. Remove the cover and bake for 15 minutes more
8. Serve and enjoy!

Nutrition (Per Serving)

- Calories: 150
- Fat: 4g
- Carbohydrates: 4g
- Protein: 25g

Onion and Bacon Pork Chops

Serving: 4

Prep Time: 10 minutes

Cook Time: 45 minutes

Ingredients:

- 2 onions, peeled and chopped
- 6 bacon slices, chopped
- ½ cup chicken stock
- Salt and pepper to taste
- 4 pork chops

How To:

1. Heat up a pan over medium heat and add bacon
2. Stir and cook until crispy
3. Transfer to bowl
4. Return pan to medium heat and add onions, season with salt and pepper
5. Stir and cook for 15 minutes
6. Transfer to the same bowl with bacon
7. Return the pan to heat (medium-high) and add pork chops
8. Season with salt and pepper and brown for 3 minutes
9. Flip and lower heat to medium
10. Cook for 7 minutes more
11. Add stock and stir cook for 2 minutes
12. Return the bacon and onions to the pan and stir cook for 1 minute
13. Serve and enjoy!

Nutrition (Per Serving)

- Calories: 325
- Fat: 18g
- Carbohydrates: 6g
- Protein: 36g

Easy Butternut Chicken

Serving: 4

Prep Time: 15 minutes

Cook Time: 30 minutes

Ingredients:

- ½ pound Nitrate free bacon
- 6 chicken thighs, boneless and skinless
- 2-3 cups butternut squash, cubed
- Extra virgin olive oil
- Fresh chopped sage
- Salt and pepper as needed

How To:

1. Prepare your oven by preheating it to 425 °F
2. Take a large skillet and place it over medium-high heat, add bacon and fry until crispy
3. Take bacon and place it on the side, crumble the bacon
4. Add cubed butternut squash in the bacon grease and Sauté, season with salt and pepper
5. Once the squash is tender, remove from the skillet and transfer to a plate
6. Add coconut oil to the skillet and add chicken thighs, cook for 10 minutes
7. Season with salt and pepper
8. Remove skillet from the stove and transfer to the oven
9. Bake for 12-15 minutes, top with crumbled bacon and sage
10. Enjoy!

Nutrition (Per Serving)

- Calories: 323
- Fat: 19g
- Carbohydrates: 8g
- Protein: 12g

Simple Mustard Chicken

Serving: 4

Prep Time: 10 minutes

Cook Time: 40 minutes

Ingredients:

- 4 chicken breasts
- ½ cup chicken broth
- 3-4 tablespoons mustard
- 3 tablespoons olive oil
- 1 teaspoon paprika
- 1 teaspoon chili powder
- 1 teaspoon garlic powder

How To:

1. Take a small bowl and mix mustard, olive oil, paprika, chicken broth, garlic powder, chicken broth, and chili
2. Add chicken breast and marinate for 30 minutes
3. Take a lined baking sheet and arrange the chicken
4. Bake for 35 minutes at 375 °F
5. Serve and enjoy!

Nutrition (Per Serving)

- Calories: 531
- Fat: 23g
- Carbohydrates: 10g
- Protein: 64g

Chapter 4: Dessert

Lemon Mousse

Serving: 4

Prep Time: 10 + chill time

Cook Time: 10 minutes

Ingredients:

- 1 cup coconut cream
- 8 ounces cream cheese, soft
- ¼ cup fresh lemon juice
- 3 pinches salt
- 1 teaspoon lemon liquid stevia

How To:

1. Preheat your oven to 350 °F
2. Grease a ramekin with butter
3. Beat cream, cream cheese, fresh lemon juice, salt and lemon liquid stevia in a mixer
4. Pour batter into ramekin
5. Bake for 10 minutes, then transfer the mousse to a serving glass
6. Let it chill for 2 hours and serve
7. Enjoy!

Nutrition (Per Serving)

- Calories: 395
- Fat: 31g
- Carbohydrates: 3g
- Protein: 5g

Jalapeno Crisp

Serving: 20

Prep Time: 10 minutes

Cook Time: 1 hour 15 minutes

Ingredients:

- 1 cup sesame seeds
- 1 cup sunflower seeds
- 1 cup flaxseeds
- ½ cup hulled hemp seeds
- 3 tablespoons Psyllium husk
- 1 teaspoon salt
- 1 teaspoon baking powder
- 2 cups of water

How To:

1. Pre-heat your oven to 350 °F
2. Take your blender and add seeds, baking powder, salt, and Psyllium husk
3. Blend well until a sand-like texture appears
4. Stir in water and mix until a batter forms
5. Allow the batter to rest for 10 minutes until a dough-like thick mixture forms
6. Pour the dough onto a cookie sheet lined with parchment paper
7. Spread it evenly, making sure that it has a thickness of ¼ inch thick all around
8. Bake for 75 minutes in your oven
9. Remove and cut into 20 spices
10. Allow them to cool for 30 minutes and enjoy!

Nutrition (Per Serving)

- Calories: 156
- Fat: 13g
- Carbohydrates: 2g
- Protein: 5g

Raspberry Popsicle

Serving: 4

Prep Time: 2 hours

Cook Time: 15 minutes

Ingredients:

- 1 ½ cups raspberries
- 2 cups of water

How To:

1. Take a pan and fill it up with water
2. Add raspberries
3. Place it over medium heat and bring to water to a boil
4. Reduce the heat and simmer for 15 minutes
5. Remove heat and pour the mix into Popsicle molds
6. Add a popsicle stick and let it chill for 2 hours
7. Serve and enjoy!

Nutrition (Per Serving)

- Calories: 58
- Fat: 0.4g
- Carbohydrates: 0g
- Protein: 1.4g

Easy Fudge

Serving: 25

Prep Time: 15 minutes + chill time

Cook Time: 5 minutes

Ingredients:

- 1 ¾ cups of coconut butter
- 1 cup pumpkin puree
- 1 teaspoon ground cinnamon
- ¼ teaspoon ground nutmeg
- 1 tablespoon coconut oil

How To:

1. Take an 8x8 inch square baking pan and line it with aluminum foil
2. Take a spoon and scoop out the coconut butter into a heated pan and allow the butter to melt
3. Keep stirring well and remove from the heat once fully melted
4. Add spices and pumpkin and keep straining until you have a grain-like texture
5. Add coconut oil and keep stirring to incorporate everything
6. Scoop the mixture into your baking pan and evenly distribute it
7. Place wax paper on top of the mixture and press gently to straighten the top
8. Remove the paper and discard
9. Allow it to chill for 1-2 hours
10. Once chilled, take it out and slice it up into pieces
11. Enjoy!

Nutrition (Per Serving)

- Calories: 120
- Fat: 10g
- Carbohydrates: 5g
- Protein: 1.2g

Blueberry Muffins

Serving: 4

Prep Time: 10 minutes

Cook Time: 30 minutes

Ingredients:

- 1 cup almond flour
- Pinch of salt
- 1/8 teaspoon baking soda
- 1 whole egg
- 2 tablespoons coconut oil, melted
- ½ cup of coconut milk
- ¼ cup fresh blueberries

How To:

1. Preheat your oven to 350 °F
2. Line a muffin tin with paper muffin cups
3. Add almond flour, salt, baking soda to a bowl and mix, keep it on the side
4. Take another bowl and add egg, coconut oil, coconut milk, and mix
5. Add mix to flour mix and gently combine until incorporated
6. Mix in blueberries and fill the cupcakes tins with batter
7. Bake for 20-25 minutes
8. Enjoy!

Nutrition (Per Serving)

- Calories: 167
- Fat: 15g
- Carbohydrates: 2.1g
- Protein: 5.2g

The Coconut Loaf

Serving: 4

Prep Time: 15 minutes

Cook Time: 40 minutes

Ingredients:

- 1 ½ tablespoons coconut flour
- ¼ teaspoon baking powder
- 1/8 teaspoon salt
- 1 tablespoon coconut oil, melted
- 1 whole egg

How To:

1. Preheat your oven to 350 °F
2. Add coconut flour, baking powder, salt
3. Add coconut oil, eggs and stir well until mixed
4. Leave the batter for several minutes
5. Pour half the batter onto the baking pan
6. Spread it to form a circle, repeat with remaining batter
7. Bake in the oven for 10 minutes
8. Once a golden brown texture comes, let it cool and serve
9. Enjoy!

Nutrition (Per Serving)

- Calories: 297
- Fat: 14g
- Carbohydrates: 15g
- Protein: 15g

Chocolate Parfait

Serving: 4

Prep Time: 2 hours

Cook Time: nil

Ingredients:

- 2 tablespoons cocoa powder
- 1 cup almond milk
- 1 tablespoon chia seeds
- Pinch of salt
- ½ teaspoon vanilla extract

How To:

1. Take a bowl and add cocoa powder, almond milk, chia seeds, vanilla extract, and stir
2. Transfer to dessert glass and place in your fridge for 2 hours
3. Serve and enjoy!

Nutrition (Per Serving)

- Calories: 130
- Fat: 5g
- Carbohydrates: 7g
- Protein: 16g

Cauliflower Bagel

Serving: 12

Prep Time: 10 minutes

Cook Time: 30 minutes

Ingredients:

- 1 large cauliflower, divided into florets and roughly chopped
- ¼ cup nutritional yeast
- ¼ cup almond flour
- ½ teaspoon garlic powder
- 1 ½ teaspoon fine sea salt
- 2 whole eggs
- 1 tablespoon sesame seeds

How To:

1. Preheat your oven to 400 °F
2. Line a baking sheet with parchment paper, keep it on the side
3. Blend cauliflower in a food processor and transfer to a bowl
4. Add nutritional yeast, almond flour, garlic powder and salt to a bowl, mix
5. Take another bowl and whisk in eggs, add to cauliflower mix
6. Give the dough a stir
7. Incorporate the mix into the egg mix
8. Make balls from the dough, making a hole using your thumb into each ball
9. Arrange them on your prepped sheet, flattening them into bagel shapes
10. Sprinkle sesame seeds and bake for half an hour
11. Remove the oven and let them cool, enjoy!

Nutrition (Per Serving)

- Calories: 152
- Fat: 10g
- Carbohydrates: 4g
- Protein: 4g

Almond Crackers

Serving: 40 crackers

Prep Time: 10 minutes

Cook Time: 20 minutes

Ingredients:

- 1 cup almond flour
- ¼ teaspoon baking soda
- ¼ teaspoon salt
- 1/8 teaspoon black pepper
- 3 tablespoons sesame seeds
- 1 egg, beaten
- Salt and pepper to taste

How To:

1. Preheat your oven to 350 °F
2. Line two baking sheets with parchment paper and keep them on the side
3. Mix the dry ingredients into a large bowl and add egg, mix well and form a dough
4. Divide dough into two balls
5. Roll out the dough between two pieces of parchment paper
6. Cut into crackers and transfer them to prep a baking sheet
7. Bake for 15-20 minutes
8. Repeat until all the dough has been used up
9. Leave crackers to cool and serve
10. Enjoy!

Nutrition (Per Serving)

- Calories: 302
- Fat: 28g
- Carbohydrates: 4g
- Protein: 9g

Cashew and Almond Butter

Serving: 1 ½ cups

Prep Time: 5 minutes

Cook Time: Nil

Ingredients:

- 1 cup almonds, blanched
- 1/3 cup cashew nuts
- 2 tablespoons coconut oil
- Salt as needed
- ½ teaspoon cinnamon

How To:

1. Preheat your oven to 350 °F
2. Bake almonds and cashews for 12 minutes
3. Let them cool
4. Transfer to a food processor and add remaining ingredients
5. Add oil and keep blending until smooth
6. Serve and enjoy!

Nutrition (Per Serving)

- Calories: 205
- Fat: 19g
- Carbohydrates: g
- Protein: 2.8g

Nut and Chia Mix

Serving: 1

Prep Time: 10 minutes

Ingredients:

- 1 tablespoon chia seeds
- 2 cups of water
- 1 ounce Macadamia nuts
- 1-2 packets Stevia, optional
- 1-ounce hazelnuts

Directions:

1. Add all the listed ingredients to a blender.
2. Blend on high until smooth and creamy.
3. Enjoy your smoothie.

Nutritional Contents:

- Calories: 452
- Fat: 43g
- Carbohydrates: 15g
- Protein: 9g

Hearty Cucumber Bites

Serving: 4

Prep Time: 5 minutes

Cook Time: nil

Ingredients:

- 1 (8 ounces) cream cheese container, low fat
- 1 tablespoon bell pepper, diced
- 1 tablespoon shallots, diced
- 1 tablespoon parsley, chopped
- 2 cucumbers
- Pepper to taste

How To:

1. Take a bowl and add cream cheese, onion, pepper, parsley
2. Peel cucumbers and cut in half
3. Remove seeds and stuff with the cheese mix
4. Cut into bite-sized portions and enjoy!

Nutrition (Per Serving)

- Calories: 85
- Fat: 4g
- Carbohydrates: 2g
- Protein: 3g

Pop Corn Bites

Serving: 4

Prep Time: 5 minutes + 20 minutes chill time

Cook Time: 2-3 minutes

Ingredients:

- 3 cups Medjool dates, chopped
- 12 ounces brewed coffee
- 1 cup pecan, chopped
- ½ cup coconut, shredded
- ½ cup of cocoa powder

How To:

1. Soak dates in warm coffee for 5 minutes
2. Remove dates from coffee and mash them, making a fine smooth mixture
3. Stir in remaining ingredients (except cocoa powder) and form small balls out of the mixture
4. Coat with cocoa powder, serve and enjoy!

Nutrition (Per Serving)

- Calories: 265
- Fat: 12g
- Carbohydrates: 43g
- Protein 3g

Hearty Almond Bread

Serving: 8

Prep Time: 15 minutes

Cook Time: 60 minutes

Ingredients:

- 3 cups almond flour
- 1 teaspoon baking soda
- 2 teaspoons baking powder
- ¼ teaspoon sunflower seeds
- ¼ cup almond milk
- ½ cup + 2 tablespoons olive oil
- 3 whole eggs

How To:

1. Preheat your oven to 300 ° F
2. Take a 9x5 inch loaf pan and grease, keep it on the side
3. Add the listed ingredients to a bowl and pour the batter into the loaf pan
4. Bake for 60 minutes
5. Once baked, remove from oven and let it cool
6. Slice and serve!

Nutrition (Per Serving)

- Calories: 277
- Fat: 21g
- Carbohydrates: 7g
- Protein: 10g

Medjool Balls

Serving: 4

Prep Time: 5 minutes + 20 minutes chill time

Cook Time: 2-3 minutes

Ingredients:

- 3 cups Medjool dates, chopped
- 12 ounces brewed coffee
- 1 cup pecan, chopped
- ½ cup coconut, shredded
- ½ cup of cocoa powder

How To:

1. Soak dates in warm coffee for 5 minutes
2. Remove dates from coffee and mash them, making a fine smooth mixture
3. Stir in remaining ingredients (except cocoa powder) and form small balls out of the mixture
4. Coat with cocoa powder, serve and enjoy!

Nutrition (Per Serving)

- Calories: 265
- Fat: 12g
- Carbohydrates: 43g
- Protein 3g

Blueberry Pudding

Serving: 4

Prep Time: 20 minutes

Cook Time: Nil

Smart Points: 0

Ingredients:

- 2 cups of frozen blueberries
- 2 teaspoon of lime zest, grated freshly
- 20 drops of liquid stevia
- ½ teaspoon of fresh ginger, grated freshly
- 4 tablespoon of fresh lime juice
- 10 tablespoon of water

Directions:

1. Add all of the listed ingredients to a blender (except blueberries) and pulse the mixture well
2. Transfer the mix into small serving bowls and chill the bowls
3. Serve with a topping of blueberries
4. Enjoy!

Nutrition (Per Serving)

- Calories: 166
- Fat: 13g
- Carbohydrates: 13g
- Protein: 1.7g

Chia Seed Pumpkin Pudding

Serving: 4

Prep Time: 10-15 minutes/ overnight chill time

Cook Time: Nil

Ingredients:

- 1 cup maple syrup
- 2 teaspoons pumpkin spice
- 1 cup pumpkin puree
- 1 ¼ cup of almond milk
- ½ cup chia seeds

How To:

1. Add all of the ingredients to a bowl and gently stir
2. Let it refrigerate overnight or for at least 15 minutes
3. Top with your desired ingredients such as blueberries, almonds, etc.
4. Serve and enjoy!

Nutrition (Per Serving)

- Calories: 230
- Fat: 10g
- Carbohydrates:22g
- Protein:11g

Parsley Souffle

Serving: 5

Prep Time: 5 minutes

Cook Time: 6 minutes

Ingredients:

- 2 whole eggs
- 1 fresh red chili pepper, chopped
- 2 tablespoons coconut cream
- 1 tablespoon fresh parsley, chopped
- Sunflower seeds to taste

How To:

1. Preheat your oven to 390 °F
2. Almond butter two soufflé dishes
3. Add the ingredients to a blender and mix well
4. Divide batter into soufflé dishes and bake for 6 minutes
5. Serve and enjoy!

Nutrition (Per Serving)

- Calories: 108
- Fat: 9g
- Carbohydrates: 9g
- Protein: 6g

Mug Cake Popper

Serving: 2

Prep Time: 5 minutes

Cook Time: 5 minutes

Ingredients:

- 2 tablespoons almond flour
- 1 tablespoon flaxseed meal
- 1 tablespoon almond butter
- 1 tablespoon cream cheese
- 1 large egg
- 1 bacon, cooked and sliced
- ½ jalapeno pepper
- ½ teaspoon baking powder
- ¼ teaspoon sunflower seeds

How To:

1. Take a frying pan and place it over medium heat
2. Add sliced bacon and cook until they have a crispy texture
3. Take a microwave proof container and mix all of the listed ingredients (including cooked bacon), clean the sides
4. Microwave for 75 seconds making sure to put your microwave to high power
5. Take out the cup and slam it against a surface to take the cake out
6. Garnish with a bit of jalapeno and serve!

Nutrition (Per Serving)

- Calories: 429
- Fat: 38g
- Carbohydrates: 6g
- Protein: 16g

Cinnamon Rice Pudding

Serving: 4

Prep Time: 10 minutes

Cooking Time: 5 hours

Ingredients:

- 6 ½ cups of water
- 1 cup brown sugar
- 2 cups white rice
- 2 cinnamon sticks
- ½ cup macadamia, shredded

Directions:

1. Add water, rice, sugar, cinnamon, and coconut to your Slow Cooker
2. Gently stir
3. Place lid and cook on HIGH for 5 hours
4. Discard cinnamon
5. Divide pudding between dessert dishes and enjoy!

Nutrition (Per Serving)

- Calories: 173
- Fat: 4g
- Carbohydrates: 9g
- Protein: 4g

Chapter 5: Juice and Smoothies
Berry Shake

Serving: 1

Prep Time: 10 minutes

Ingredients:

- ½ cup whole milk yogurt
- ¼ cup raspberries
- ¼ cup blackberry
- ¼ cup strawberries, chopped
- 1 tablespoon cocoa powder
- 1 ½ cups of water

Directions:

1. Add listed ingredients to a blender

2. Blend until you have a smooth and creamy texture

3. Serve chilled and enjoy!

Nutrition (Per Serving)

- Calories: 255
- Fat: 19g
- Carbohydrates: 20g
- Protein: 6g

Watermelon Sorbet

Serving: 4

Prep Time: 20 minutes + 20 hours chill time

Cook Time: Nil

Ingredients:

- 4 cups watermelons, seedless and chunked
- ¼ cup of coconut sugar
- 2 tablespoons of lime juice

Directions:

1. Add the listed ingredients to a blender and puree
2. Transfer to a freezer container with a tight-fitting lid
3. Freeze the mix for about 4-6 hours until you have gelatin-like consistency
4. Puree the mix once again in batches and return to the container
5. Chill overnight
6. Allow the sorbet to stand for 5 minutes before serving and enjoy!

Nutrition (Per Serving)

- Calories: 91
- Fat: 0g
- Carbohydrates: 25g
- Protein: 1g

Berry Smoothie

Serving: 2

Prep Time: 4 minutes

Cook Time: 0 minutes

Ingredients:

- ¼ cup of frozen blueberries
- ¼ cup of frozen blackberries
- 1 cup of unsweetened almond milk
- 1 teaspoon of vanilla bean extract
- 3 teaspoon of flaxseed
- 1 scoop of chilled Greek yogurt
- Stevia as needed

How To:

1. Mix everything in a blender and emulsify.
2. Pulse the mixture four-times until you have your desired thickness.
3. Pour the mixture into a glass and enjoy!

Nutrition (Per Serving)

- Calories: 221
- Fat: 9g
- Protein: 21g
- Carbohydrates: 10g

Berry and Almond Smoothie

Serving: 4

Prep Time: 10 minutes

Cook Time: nil

Ingredients:

- 1 cup of blueberries, frozen
- 1 whole banana
- ½ a cup of almond milk
- 1 tablespoon of almond butter
- Water as needed

How To:

1. Add the listed ingredients to your blender and blend well until you have a smoothie-like texture
2. Chill and serve
3. Enjoy!

Nutrition (Per Serving)

- Calories: 321
- Fat: 11g
- Carbohydrates: 55g
- Protein: 5g

Mango and Pear Smoothie

Serving: 1

Prep Time: 10 minutes

Cook Time: Nil

Ingredients:

- 1 ripe mango, cored and chopped
- ½ mango, peeled, pitted and chopped
- 1 cup kale, chopped
- ½ cup plain Greek yogurt
- 2 ice cubes

How To:

1. Add pear, mango, yogurt, kale, and mango to a blender and puree
2. Add ice and blend until you have a smooth texture
3. Serve and enjoy!

Nutrition (Per Serving)

- Calories: 293
- Fat: 8g
- Carbohydrates: 53g
- Protein: 8g

Pineapple Juice

Serving: 4

Prep Time: 10 minutes

Cook Time: nil

Ingredients:

- 4 cups of fresh pineapple, chopped
- 1 pinch of sunflower seeds
- 1 ½ cup of water

How To:

1. Add the listed ingredients to your blender and blend well until you have a smoothie-like texture
2. Chill and serve
3. Enjoy!

Nutrition (Per Serving)

- Calories: 82
- Fat: 0.2g
- Carbohydrates: 21g
- Protein: 21

Coffee Smoothie

Serving: 1

Prep Time: 10 minutes

Ingredients:

- 1 tablespoon chia seeds
- 2 cups strongly brewed coffee, chilled
- 1 ounce Macadamia nuts
- 1-2 packets Stevia, optional
- 1 tablespoon MCT oil

Directions:

1. Add all the listed ingredients to a blender

2. Blend on high until smooth and creamy

3. Enjoy your smoothie

Nutritional Contents:

- Calories: 395
- Fat: 39g
- Carbohydrates: 11g
- Protein: 5.2g

Blackberry and Apple Smoothie

Serving: 2

Prep Time: 5 minutes

Ingredients:

- 2 cups frozen blackberries
- ½ cup apple cider
- 1 apple, cubed
- 2/3 cup non-fat lemon yogurt

Cooking Directions

1. Add the listed ingredients to your blender and blend until smooth
2. Serve chilled!

Nutrition (Per Serving)

- Calories: 200
- Fat: 10g
- Carbohydrates: 14g
- Protein 2g

Minty Cherry Smoothie

Serving: 2

Prep Time: 5 minutes

Ingredients:

- ¾ cup cherries
- 1 teaspoon mint
- ½ cup almond milk
- ½ cup kale
- ½ teaspoon fresh vanilla

Cooking Directions:

1. Wash and cut cherries
2. Take the pits out
3. Add cherries to the blender
4. Pour almond milk
5. Wash the mint and put two sprigs in blender
6. Separate the kale leaves from the stems
7. Put kale in a blender
8. Press vanilla bean and cut lengthwise with a knife
9. Scoop out your desired amount of vanilla and add to the blender
10. Blend until smooth
11. Serve chilled and enjoy!

Nutrition (Per Serving)

- Calories: 200
- Fat: 10g
- Carbohydrates: 14g
- Protein 2g

Fruit Smoothie

Serving: 1

Prep Time: 10 minutes

Ingredients:

- 1 cup spring mix salad blend
- 2 cups of water
- 3 medium blackberries, whole
- 1 packet Stevia, optional
- 1 tablespoon coconut flakes shredded and unsweetened
- 2 tablespoons pecans, chopped
- 1 tablespoon hemp seed
- 1 tablespoon sunflower seed

Directions:

1. Add all the listed ingredients to a blender
2. Blend on high until smooth and creamy
3. Enjoy your smoothie

Nutrition (Per Serving)

- Calories: 385
- Fat: 34g
- Carbohydrates: 16g
- Protein: 6.9g

The Green Minty Smoothie

Serving: 1

Prep Time: 10 minutes

Ingredients:

- 1 stalk celery
- 2 cups of water
- 2 ounces almonds
- 1 packet Stevia
- 2 mint leaves

Directions:

1. Add listed ingredients to a blender
2. Blend until you have a smooth and creamy texture
3. Serve chilled and enjoy!

Nutrition (Per Serving)

- Calories: 417
- Fat: 43g
- Carbohydrates: 10g
- Protein: 5.5g

Mocha Milk Shake

Serving: 1

Prep Time: 10 minutes

Ingredients:

- 1 cup whole milk
- 2 tablespoons cocoa powder
- 2 pack stevia
- 1 cup brewed coffee, chilled
- 1 tablespoon coconut oil

Directions:

1. Add listed ingredients to a blender
2. Blend until you have a smooth and creamy texture
3. Serve chilled and enjoy!

Nutrition (Per Serving)

- Calories: 293
- Fat: 23g
- Carbohydrates: 19g
- Protein: 10g

Gut Cleansing Smoothie

Serving: 1

Prep Time: 10 minutes

Ingredients:

- 1 ½ tablespoons coconut oil, unrefined
- ½ cup plain full-fat yogurt
- 1 tablespoon chia seeds
- 1 serving aloe vera leaves
- ½ cup frozen blueberries, unsweetened
- 1 tablespoon hemp hearts
- 1 cup of water
- 1 scoop Pinnaclife prebiotic fiber

Directions:

1. Add listed ingredients to a blender
2. Blend until you have a smooth and creamy texture
3. Serve chilled and enjoy!

Nutrition (Per Serving)

- Calories: 409
- Fat: 33g
- Carbohydrates: 8g
- Protein: 12g

Cabbage and Chia Glass

Serving: 2

Prep Time: 10 minutes

Ingredients:

- 1/3 cup cabbage
- 1 cup cold unsweetened almond milk
- 1 tablespoon chia seeds
- ½ cup cherries
- ½ cup lettuce

Directions:

1. Add coconut milk to your blender
2. Cut cabbage and add to your blender
3. Place chia seeds in a coffee grinder and chop to powder, brush the powder into a blender
4. Pit the cherries and add them to the blender
5. Wash and dry the lettuce and chop
6. Add to the mix
7. Cover and blend on low followed by medium
8. Taste the texture and serve chilled!

Nutrition (Per Serving)

- Calories: 409
- Fat: 33g
- Carbohydrates: 8g
- Protein: 12g

Blueberry and Kale Mix

Serving: 1

Prep Time: 10 minutes

Ingredients:

- ½ cup low-fat Greek Yogurt
- 1 cup baby kale greens
- 1 pack stevia
- 1 tablespoon MCT oil
- ¼ cup blueberries
- 1 tablespoon pepitas
- 1 tablespoon flaxseed, ground
- 1 ½ cups of water

Directions:

1. Add listed ingredients to a blender

2. Blend until you have a smooth and creamy texture

3. Serve chilled and enjoy!

Nutrition (Per Serving)

- Calories: 307
- Fat: 24g
- Carbohydrates: 14g
- Protein: 9g

Rosemary and Lemon Garden Smoothie

Serving: 1

Prep Time: 10 minutes

Ingredients:

- ½ cup low-fat Greek Yogurt
- 1 cup garden greens
- 1 pack stevia
- 1 tablespoon olive oil
- 1 stalk fresh rosemary
- 1 tablespoon lemon juice, fresh
- 1 tablespoon pepitas
- 1 tablespoon flaxseed, ground
- 1 ½ cups of water

Directions:

1. Add listed ingredients to a blender
2. Blend until you have a smooth and creamy texture
3. Serve chilled and enjoy!

Nutrition (Per Serving)

- Calories: 312
- Fat: 25g
- Carbohydrates: 14g
- Protein: 9g

Melon and Coconut Dish

Serving: 1

Prep Time: 10 minutes

Ingredients:

- ¼ cup low-fat Greek yogurt
- 1 pack stevia
- 1 tablespoon coconut oil
- ½ cup melon, sliced
- 1 tablespoon coconut flakes, unsweetened
- 1 tablespoon chia seeds
- 1 and ½ cups of water

Directions:

1. Add listed ingredients to a blender

2. Blend until you have a smooth and creamy texture

3. Serve chilled and enjoy!

Nutrition (Per Serving)

- Calories: 278
- Fat: 21g
- Carbohydrates: 15g
- Protein: 6g

Strawberry Glass

Serving: 2

Prep Time: 10 minutes

Ingredients:

- 1-2 handful baby greens
- 3 medium kale leaves
- 5-8 mint leaves
- 1-inch piece ginger, peeled
- 1 avocado
- 1 cup strawberries
- 6-8 ounces coconut water + 6-8 ounces filtered water
- Fresh juice of one lime
- 1-2 teaspoon olive oil

Directions:

1. Add listed ingredients to a blender
2. Blend until you have a smooth and creamy texture
3. Serve chilled and enjoy!

Nutrition (Per Serving)

- Calories: 409
- Fat: 33g
- Carbohydrates: 8g
- Protein: 12g

Ginger Strawberry Shake

Serving: 1

Prep Time: 10 minutes

Ingredients:

- 1 cup almond milk
- ½ teaspoon ginger powder
- 1 small stalk celery
- 1 cup spring salad mix
- 1 teaspoon sesame seeds
- 1 cup of water
- 1 pack Stevia

Directions:

1. Add listed ingredients to a blender

2. Blend until you have a smooth and creamy texture

3. Serve chilled and enjoy!

Nutrition (Per Serving)

- Calories: 475
- Fat: 50g
- Carbohydrates: 10g
- Protein: 7g

Almond and Kale Extreme

Serving: 1

Prep Time: 10 minutes

Ingredients:

- ¼ cup kale, torn
- 2 cups of water
- 2-Oz almonds
- 1 packet Stevia, if desired
- ½ cup spinach, packed

Directions:

1. Soak almonds in water and keep it overnight.
2. Do not discard water and add all in a blender.
3. Add all the listed ingredients to a blender.
4. Blend on high until smooth and creamy.
5. Enjoy your smoothie.

Nutrition (Per Serving)

- Calories: 334
- Fat: 28g
- Carbohydrates: 14g
- Protein: 12g

Conclusion

I am honored to think that you found my book interesting and informative enough to read it all through to the end.

I thank you again for purchasing this book, and I hope that you had as much fun reading it as I had writing it.

I bid you farewell and encourage you to move forward with your Renal Diet journey!

Made in the USA
Columbia, SC
30 September 2020